U0462937

开心大冒险

Ick's Bleh Day

[美]威力·布莱文斯/著　[美]吉姆·帕约/绘

王婧/译

电子工业出版社

Publishing House of Electronics Industry

北京·BEIJING

本书中文简体版专有出版权由Red Chair Press LLC通过CA-Link International LLC授予电子工业出版社，未经许可，不得以任何方式复制或抄袭本书的任何部分。

版权贸易合同登记号　图字：01-2022-0735

图书在版编目（CIP）数据

开心大冒险 / (美) 威力·布莱文斯 (Wiley Blevins) 著；(美) 吉姆·帕约 (Jim Paillot) 绘；王婧译.
－－ 北京：电子工业出版社，2023.6
（胖狗和瘦狗）
ISBN 978-7-121-44941-3

Ⅰ. ①开… Ⅱ. ①威… ②吉… ③王… Ⅲ. ①儿童故事－图画故事－美国－现代 Ⅳ. ①I712.85

中国国家版本馆CIP数据核字(2023)第077352号

责任编辑：范丽鹏
印　　刷：天津图文方嘉印刷有限公司
装　　订：天津图文方嘉印刷有限公司
出版发行：电子工业出版社
　　　　　北京市海淀区万寿路173信箱　邮编：100036
开　　本：787×1092　1/16　印张：26.25　字数：264千字
版　　次：2023年6月第1版
印　　次：2023年6月第1次印刷
定　　价：208.00元(全8册)

凡所购买电子工业出版社图书有缺损问题，请向购买书店调换。若书店售缺，请与本社发行部联系，联系及邮购电话：(010) 88254888，88258888。
质量投诉请发邮件至zlts@phei.com.cn，盗版侵权举报请发邮件至dbqq@phei.com.cn。
本书咨询联系方式：(010) 88254161 转 1862，fanlp@phei.com.cn。

目录

闪亮登场的主角们

克鲁德

艾克

绒球小姐

鲍勃

在泥地里撒欢儿！

"你怎么了，艾克？"克鲁德问。

"我觉得自己很**'卜啦'**。"艾克说。

"**'卜啦?**"克鲁德不明白。

"是的，"艾克说，"就是伤心、沮丧、超级无聊的意思。"

"哦，"克鲁德说，"那我们就把好心情找回来吧，你应该像我一样开朗起来，哥们儿！"

"嗯，"艾克想了想说，"要是像克鲁德一样，应该感觉很棒吧！"

1

　　"让我想想怎样才能让你开心起来呢？"克鲁德说，"要不然给你来块骨头吧？"

　　"不，"艾克说，"我一点儿都不想要骨头。"

　　"那你想不想去追松鼠玩儿？"克鲁德问。

　　"不，"艾克说，"我一点儿都不想去追松鼠玩儿。"

"那你想不想看我跳个舞？"克鲁德又问。

"不，"艾克说，"我一点儿都不想看你跳舞，而且没有任何人想看你跳舞。"

"那你想不想吃个冰激凌？"克鲁德问。

艾克立马坐了起来，说："这倒是个好主意。"

"那我们还等什么呢。"克鲁德说。

于是克鲁德和艾克立刻朝着总是能吃到冰激凌的地方，也就是公园出发啦！

　　他们穿过自家的院子，再跳过围栏，然后落在了马丁太太的院子里。啪唧一声！俩人溅了一身的泥巴！

　　"这可不是冰激凌哦，"艾克说，"不过黏糊糊的也挺好玩儿的。"

　　"那你现在是不是没有那么'卜啦'了呀？"克鲁德问。

　　艾克摇了摇头："也就好了那么一点点。"

　　"那咱们还是继续出发吧。"克鲁德说。

　　就在这时，突然有什么东西从他们头顶上方走过。俩人立马呆住了。

　　"我都听你的。"艾克小声说。

克鲁德和艾克同时抬头向上看去。绒球小姐正坐在围栏上，她的尾巴甩来甩去，像在舔棒棒糖似的轮流舔着自己的两只爪子。

　　"你们两个简直是**臭气熏天**。"绒球小姐咕哝着。

　　"我们怎么了？"艾克问。

　　"**臭气**……哦，当我没说过吧。"绒球小姐说，"你们两个家伙就不能把自己弄得干净些吗？就像我这样！"

　　"也许等一会儿会下雨吧。"艾克说。

　　克鲁德抬头看了看晴朗无云的蓝天："或者，也许不会。"

绒球小姐抬起她高傲的脑袋，这时，一道明晃晃的亮光从她脖子上戴着的什么东西上反射了过来。

　　"那是什么呀？"艾克问。

　　"你晃到我们了。"克鲁德说。

　　"这是我的新项圈，"绒球小姐娇傲地说，"是真正的钻石哦！"她站起身来，大摇大摆地在围栏上走来走去炫耀着。"我的主人从巴黎给我买的，你们也想要吧？"

　　克鲁德忍不住翻了个大白眼儿。

　　“我们的项圈是鲍勃在我家附近的地方买的。”艾克说。

　　“我们的项圈是鲍勃自己做的。”克鲁德小声提醒。

　　绒球小姐大笑了起来，她故意摇了摇头，脖子上的钻石项圈在阳光下闪闪发亮。

　　“嘿！艾克，”克鲁德说，“想不想玩个更有趣的？”

　　“想呀！”艾克答道。

　　“那你就摇晃起来。”克鲁德说。

　　“摇晃起来？”艾克疑惑地问。

　　“没错，”克鲁德说，“就好像地震了似的摇晃起来。”

艾克立马开始摇晃起身体，他身上的泥巴瞬间被甩了出去。

噼里啪啦的一阵"泥巴雨"！绒球小姐嘴里发出愤怒地哈气声，飞快地跑开了。

"抱歉啦！"艾克大声喊。

"就一点点而已。"克鲁德小声说。

"你现在是不是没有那么'**卜啦**'了呀？"克鲁德问。

艾克摇了摇头："也就好了那么一点点。"

"等我们到了公园就会好啦！"克鲁德说。

咕噜，咕噜，咕噜！

　　克鲁德和艾克沿着大街蹦蹦跳跳地继续前进，他们先是绕过一个拐角，然后在一个巨大的垃圾桶旁边停了下来。他们闻了闻垃圾桶，又闻了闻散落在垃圾桶四周的垃圾，然后俩人互相闻了闻对方。**嗅啊，嗅啊，确实有点儿臭！**

待售

　　艾克和克鲁德闻完，朝着另一条街道跑去，他们绕过另一个拐角，来到了公园。艾克和克鲁德一个"急刹车"停了下来。克鲁德朝着四周望去，问道："跑哪儿去了呀？"

　　"什么东西哪儿去了？"艾克问。

　　"粉色的大卡车呀！"克鲁德说，"就是那辆冰激凌车。"

　　"它不在这儿，"艾克问，"那我们接下来做什么呢？我还是感觉很'卜啦'呀！"

　　克鲁德站着开始思索起来。要是他此刻能够吃到冰激凌的话，思考起来肯定会容易很多。

　　"我有主意了，"克鲁德说，"我们来玩扮演鲍勃的游戏怎么样？"

　　"好呀，"艾克说，"扮演鲍勃一定很有趣，但是你要怎么扮演鲍勃呢？"

　　"我说出一个命令，"克鲁德说，"然后你按照这个命令去执行。"

　　"那一定很好玩儿！"艾克说。

　　"那我们就开始吧。"克鲁德说完，叼起一根木棍然后扔了出去，大声喊道："接住它！"艾克朝着木棍追去，跑进了高高的草丛里……

这时，一只蝴蝶拍打着翅膀从艾克的头顶飞过。艾克一下被它吸引住了，他停下脚步，盯着蝴蝶黑色和橘色相间的翅膀，由衷地赞美道："你可真漂亮啊！"艾克打了个滚儿躺在草地上，看见蝴蝶朝他飞了下来，然后落在他的鼻头上。"真漂亮啊！"艾克又说了一遍。

　　"嘿，艾克，"克鲁德叫道，"你有没有捡到那根木棍啊？"

　　"木棍？"艾克疑惑地坐了起来。

　　"对啊，就是我刚刚扔的那根木棍。"克鲁德说。

　　"哦，那根木棍，"艾克说，"它在哪儿呢？"克鲁德指了指。艾克爬过草丛，朝四周看了看。

　　这边有根木棍，那边还有根木棍，到处都是一根根的木棍，但唯独没有克鲁德刚才扔的**那根**木棍。"别管它啦！"克鲁德说道。

　　艾克朝着克鲁德跑了回来，"让我们再玩一遍吧。"艾克说。

　　"没问题，"克鲁德说，"打个滚儿，然后汪汪叫。"

　　"你说话的语气可真像鲍勃啊。"艾克说。

　　"快做呀！"克鲁德有点着急。

　　艾克立马按照克鲁德的指令做了起来。他朝着右边滚滚，又朝左边滚滚，他滚啊滚啊……

艾克朝着山下滚了下去，滚啊滚啊滚，一直滚到了小池塘的边上才停了下来。

"呱呱，呱呱，呱呱"。"那是什么？"艾克问。克鲁德跑到他的身边。"呱呱，呱呱，呱呱呱"。

这时，水塘里突然冒出来两只眼睛。"怪物啊！"艾克大叫一声，跳到了克鲁德的背上。

"快下来。"克鲁德边说边前前后后、左左右右、上上下下地不停摇晃起来。

19

啪唧一声！他们一同掉进了小池塘里。咕噜……
咕噜……咕噜，艾克从水里冒了出来。

　　"呱呱"，一只青蛙从艾克脑袋上跳了下去。
"再见，青蛙。"艾克说，"你很漂亮，一点儿也不
像怪物。"

　　这时，克鲁德也从水里冒了出来。"呱呱呱"，一只青蛙坐在了他的脸上，克鲁德一把把它扒拉下去。

　　"哈哈，至少我们现在很干净啦。"艾克说。

　　"所以，"克鲁德问，"你现在是不是没有那么'卜啦'了呀？"

　　艾克摇了摇头："也就好了那么一点点。"

　　克鲁德叹了口气，可紧接着他就听到了一阵喧闹声，而且正是他期盼已久的喧闹声。

做好准备！

"你听到叮咚叮咚的笛声了吗？"克鲁德问。

"听到了，"艾克说，"那是什么声音？"

"那是冰激凌车的笛声呀，"克鲁德说，"冲呀！"他们朝山上飞奔过去，穿过高高的草丛，然后来到粉色大卡车的旁边。

一个又高又瘦的男人正从冰激凌车里往外递着各式各样的圆筒冰激凌：有超大的、超小的，还有撒着各式糖霜的。高瘦男人并没有把冰激凌递给克鲁德和艾克，因为他根本就没有看到他俩。

　　"那我们现在该怎么办？"艾克问。

　　"我们站到一个孩子的旁边，"克鲁德悄悄地说，"年龄越小越好。"

　　"为什么呀？"艾克不太明白。

　　"他们是最容易把手里的冰激凌掉在地上的人。"克鲁德解释道。

　　"那然后呢？"艾克继续问。

　　"然后你要像自己的舌头着火了一样，赶快去舔冰激凌呀！"克鲁德说。

　　"明白，"艾克说，"我的舌头已经准备好啦！"

24

于是，艾克朝着一个个子矮矮的小男孩儿跑了过去。艾克抬起头来，小男孩儿正在舔着他的冰激凌。"一定很好吃。"艾克心里嘀咕着。

"肯定特别好吃。"克鲁德也在心里嘀咕着，然后他故意大声叫了起来。

小男孩儿被吓了一跳，手里的冰激凌一下掉在了地上。"哇——"

"计谋成功。"克鲁德欢呼起来。

艾克立马朝着掉在地上的冰激凌冲了过去，他的舌头已经准备好要舔上去了。

"哇——"艾克叼起掉在地上的圆筒冰激凌，他抬头看了看大哭的小男孩儿，"哦，不，"艾克心想，"他怎么感觉好像比我还要'卜啦'呢！"

艾克没有吃掉到嘴边的圆筒冰激凌，他选择把冰激凌递给那个小男孩儿。小男孩儿拿起圆筒冰激凌开心地继续舔了起来。

　　这时，那个又高又瘦的男人从冰激凌车里探出头来，他想看看男孩儿为什么要哭，结果一眼便发现了克鲁德和艾克，他大吼道："走开！"

　　"快跑！"克鲁德大声喊道。

　　他们绕过粉色的冰激凌卡车，从公园的长凳后面跑过，又沿着自行车道跑到了人行横道，随后脚下一个"急刹车"停了下来。

　　"那个冰激凌……抱歉啦。"克鲁德说。

　　"你不用对我道歉。"艾克说。

　　"不用？"克鲁德问。

　　"是的，"艾克说，"我已经不再感觉'卜啦'了，现在我觉得我像是艾克了。"

　　"像是艾克？"克鲁德不解地问。

　　"是的，"艾克说道，"我感觉我又变回了我自己。"

　　"这简直太棒了，"克鲁德开心地说，"那我们回家去吧，哥们儿！"

于是克鲁德和艾克两人一路闻闻嗅嗅，
愉快地走回了家。

英文原文

Meet the Characters

Crud

Ick

Miss Puffy

Bob

Fun in the Mud

"What's wrong, Ick?" asked Crud.

"I'm feeling *bleh*," said Ick.

"*Bleh*?" asked Crud.

"Yes," said Ick. "Sad. Bad. Bored."

"Oh," said Crud. "Then we need to fix that. You need to feel good like me, buddy."

"Hmmm," thought Ick. "It would be great to feel like Crud."

在泥地里撒欢儿！

"你怎么了，艾克？"克鲁德问。

"我觉得自己很'卜咧'。"艾克说。

"'卜咧'？"克鲁德不明白。

"是的，"艾克说，"就是伤心、沮丧、超级无聊的意思。"

"哦，"克鲁德说，"那我们就把好心情找回来吧，你应该像我一样开朗起来，哥们儿！"

"嗯，"艾克想了想说，"要是像克鲁德一样，应该感觉很棒吧！"

1

2

"那你想不想看我跳个舞？"克鲁德又问。

"不，"艾克说，"我一点儿都不想看你跳舞，而且没有任何人想看你跳舞。"

"那你想不想吃个冰激凌？"克鲁德问。

艾克立马坐了起来，说："这倒是个好主意。"

"那我们还等什么呢。"克鲁德说。

"让我想想怎样才能让你开心起来呢？"克鲁德说，"要不然给你来块骨头吧？"

"不，"艾克说，"我一点儿都不想要骨头。"

"那你想不想去追松鼠玩儿？"克鲁德问。

"不，"艾克说，"我一点儿都不想去追松鼠玩儿。"

3

"Let me think of a way to cheer you up," said Crud. "Would you like a dog bone?"

"No," said Ick. "I would not like a dog bone."

"Would you like to chase a squirrel?" asked Crud.

"No," said Ick. "I would not like to chase a squirrel."

"Would you like to see me dance?" asked Crud.

"No," said Ick. "I would not like to see you dance. No one would."

"Then what about some ice cream?" asked Crud.

Ick sat up. "I think I would like that," he said.

"Then let's get some," said Crud.

于是克鲁德和艾克立刻朝着总是能吃到冰激凌的地方，也就是公园出发啦！

他们穿过自家的院子，再跳过围栏，然后落在了马丁太太的院子里。啪唧一声！俩人溅了一身的泥巴！

"这可不是冰激凌哦，"艾克说，"不过黏糊糊的也挺好玩儿的。"

"那你现在是不是没有那么'卜唠'了呀？"克鲁德问。

艾克摇了摇头："也就好了那么一点点。"

"那咱们还是继续出发吧。"克鲁德说。

就在这时，突然有什么东西从他们头顶上方走过。俩人立马呆住了。

"我都听你的。"艾克小声说。

4

5

Ick and Crud set off for the one place that always had ice cream. The park.

They raced through their yard, jumped over the fence, and landed in Mrs. Martin's yard. Splat! Mud flew everywhere.

"This is not ice cream," said Ick. "But it is gooey and fun."

"Do you feel less *bleh* now?" asked Crud.

Ick shook his head. "Only a little."

"Then let's keep going," said Crud.

Just then something moved above them. The two froze.

"I will if you will," whispered Ick.

克鲁德和艾克同时抬头向上看去。绒球小姐正坐在围栏上，她的尾巴甩来甩去，像在舔棒棒糖似的轮流舔着自己的两只爪子。

"你们两个简直是臭气熏天。"绒球小姐咕哝着。

"我们怎么了？"艾克问。

"臭气……哦，当我没说过吧。"绒球小姐说，"你们两个家伙就不能把自己弄得干净些吗？就像我这样！"

"也许等一会儿会下雨吧。"艾克说。

克鲁德抬头看了看晴朗无云的蓝天："或者，也许不会。"

6

Ick and Crud slowly looked up. Miss Puffy sat on the fence. Her tail flipped from side to side. She licked her paws like they were lollipops.

"You two are *dis-gust-ing*," she purred.

"We're what?" asked Ick.

"*Dis... gust...* oh, never mind," said Miss Puffy. "How will you two ever get clean? Like me."

"Maybe it will rain again," said Ick.

Crud looked up at the now clear blue sky. "Or maybe not," he said.

Miss Puffy lifted her head. The light bounced off something on her neck.

"What's that?" asked Ick.

"You're blinding us," said Crud.

"It's my new collar," said Miss Puffy. "Real diamonds." She stood and strutted up and down the fence. "My owner bought it in Paris. Do you like?"

Crud rolled his eyes.

"Bob bought our collars closer to home," said Ick.

"Bob made our collars," whispered Crud.

Miss Puffy laughed. Then she shook her head so her diamond collar sparkled in the light.

"Hey Ick," whispered Crud. "Wanna have even more fun?"

"Yes!" said Ick.

"Then shake," said Crud.

"Shake?" asked Ick.

"Yes," said Crud. "Shake like an earthquake."

So Ick shook. And off flew the mud.

Fling! Sling! Splash! Miss Puffy hissed and dashed away.

"Sorry," yelled Ick.

"Sort of," whispered Crud.

"Do you feel less *bleh* now?" asked Crud.

Ick shook his head. "Only a little."

"Wait until we get to the park," said Crud.

Glub, Glub, Glub

Ick and Crud skipped down the street, around the corner, and past the big trash cans. They stopped to sniff the cans, the trash around the cans, and then each other. *Sniff. Sniff. What a whiff!*

咕噜，咕噜，咕噜！

克鲁德和艾克沿着大街蹦蹦跳跳地继续前进，他们先是绕过一个拐角，然后在一个巨大的垃圾桶旁边停了下来。他们闻了闻垃圾桶，又闻了闻散落在垃圾桶四周的垃圾，然后俩人互相闻了闻对方。哎呀，哎呀，确实有点儿臭！

11

艾克和克鲁德闻完，朝着另一条街道跑去，他们绕过另一个拐角，来到了公园。艾克和克鲁德一个"急刹车"停了下来。克鲁德朝着四周望去，问道："跑哪儿去了呀？"

"什么东西哪儿去了？"艾克问。

"粉色的大卡车呀！"克鲁德说，"就是那辆冰激凌车。"

"它不在这儿，"艾克问，"那我们接下来做什么呢？我还是感觉很🍦呀！"

克鲁德站着开始思索起来。要是他此刻能够吃到冰激凌的话，思考起来肯定会容易很多。

When they were finished sniffing, they ran down another street, around another corner, and into the park. They both skidded to a stop. Crud looked all around. "Where is it?" he asked.

"Where is what?" asked Ick.

"The big pink truck," said Crud. "With all the ice cream."

"It's not here," said Ick. "What do we do now? I still feel *bleh*."

Crud stopped to think, which is easier to do when you have ice cream in your belly.

时，一只蝴蝶拍打着翅膀从艾克的头顶飞过。艾克一下被它吸引住了，他停下脚步，盯着蝴蝶黑色和橘色相间的翅膀，由衷地赞美道："你可真漂亮啊！"于是扑个滚儿，翻在草地上，看见蝴蝶朝他飞了下来，然后落在他的鼻尖上。"真漂亮啊！"艾克又说了一遍。

"我有主意了，"克鲁德说，"我们来玩扮演鲍勃的游戏怎么样？"

"好呀，"艾克说，"扮演鲍勃一定很有趣，但是你要怎么扮演鲍勃呢？"

"我说出一个命令，"克鲁德说，"然后你按照这个命令去执行。"

"那一定很好玩儿！"艾克说。

"那我们就开始吧。"克鲁德说完，叼起一根木棍然后扔了出去，大声喊道："接住它！"艾克朝着木棍追去，跑进了高高的草丛里……

14   15

"I've got it!" said Crud. "Would you like to play Bob?"

"Okay," said Ick. "It's fun to play Bob. How do you play Bob again?"

"I give an order," said Crud. "And you do what I say."

"That is fun!" said Ick.

"Okay," said Crud. He put a stick in his mouth and tossed it away. "Fetch!" yelled Crud. Ick ran after the stick. He ran into the tall grasses until a butterfly flapped above him.

He stopped to look at its black and orange wings. "You're so pretty," Ick said. Then he rolled on his back and watched the butterfly dip down and land on his nose. "So pretty," said Ick again.

"嘿，艾克，"克鲁德叫道，"你有没有捡到那根木棍啊？"

"木棍？"艾克疑惑地坐了起来。

"对啊，就是我刚刚扔的那根木棍。"克鲁德说。

"哦，那根木棍，"艾克说，"它在哪儿呢？"克鲁德指了指。艾克爬过草丛，朝四周看了看。

这边有根木棍，那边还有根木棍，到处都是一根根的木棍，但唯独没有克鲁德刚才扔的那根木棍。"别管它啦！"克鲁德说道。

16

艾克朝着克鲁德跑了回来，"让我们再玩一遍吧。"艾克说。

"没问题，"克鲁德说，"打个滚儿，然后汪汪叫。"

"你说话的语气可真像鲍勃啊。"艾克说。

"快做呀！"克鲁德有点着急。

艾克立马按照克鲁德的指令做了起来。他朝着右边滚滚，又朝左边滚滚，他滚啊滚啊……

17

"Hey Ick," yelled Crud. "Did you get the stick?"

"Stick?" asked Ick. He sat up.

"Yes. The stick I threw," said Crud.

"Oh, that stick," said Ick. "Where is it?" Crud pointed. Ick crawled through the grass and looked all around.

Here a stick. There a stick. Everywhere a stick-stick. But not his stick. "Never mind," said Crud.

Ick ran back to Crud. "Let's try again," Ick said.

"Okay," said Crud. "Roll over and bark."

"You sound just like Bob," said Ick.

"So do it," said Crud.

Ick did. He rolled to the right. Then he rolled to the left. He rolled and rolled and rolled until…

…he rolled right down the hill. And he rolled and rolled and rolled until he stopped at the edge of a small pond.

Croak… croak… croak. "What was that?" asked Ick. Crud ran to him. *Croak… croak… ribbit.*

Two eyes popped out of the water. "A monster!" yelled Ick. Ick jumped on Crud's back.

"Get off," said Crud. Crud swayed back and forth, and forth and back, and side to side, and up and down.

啪啪一声！他们一同掉进了小池塘里。咕噜……咕噜……咕噜，艾克从水里冒了出来。

"呱呱"，一只青蛙从艾克脑袋上跳了下去。

"再见，青蛙。"艾克说，"你很漂亮，一点儿也不像怪物。"

这时，克鲁德也从水里冒了出来。"呱呱呱"，一只青蛙坐在了他的脸上，克鲁德一把把它扒拉下去。

"哈哈，至少我们现在很干净啦。"艾克说。

"所以，"克鲁德问，"你现在是不是没有那么卜啦了呀？"

艾克摇摇头："也就好了那么一点点。"

克鲁德叹了口气，可紧接着他就听到了一阵喧闹声，而且正是他期盼已久的喧闹声。

SPLAT! The two fell into the pond. Glub… glub… glub. Ick popped out of the water.

Croak. A frog jumped off his head. "Goodbye, frog," said Ick. "You're so pretty. And nothing like a monster."

Then Crud popped out of the water. *Ribbit.* A frog sat on his face. He peeled it off.

"Well at least we're clean now," said Ick.

"And?" asked Crud. "Do you feel less *bleh*?"

Ick shook his head. "Only a little."

Crud sighed. But then he heard a noise. The noise he had been waiting for.

Get Ready!

"Do you hear that ding-dong-ding-a-gong?" asked Crud.

"Yes," said Ick. "What is it?"

"It's the ice cream truck's bell," said Crud. "Run!" The two raced up the hill, through the tall grasses, and to the side of the big pink truck.

A tall, thin man handed out ice cream cones. Big ones. Little ones. And ones with sprinkles. But he didn't give Ick and Crud one. He didn't even seem to see them.

"What do we do now?" asked Ick.

"Stand next to a kid," whispered Crud. "The smaller, the better."

"Why?" asked Ick.

"They are the first to drop their cones," said Crud.

"Then what?" asked Ick.

"Then you lick like your tongue is on fire."

"Got it," said Ick. "My tongue is ready."

于是，艾克朝着一个个子矮矮的小男孩儿跑了
过去。艾克抬起头来，小男孩儿正在舔着他的冰激
凌。"一定很好吃。"艾克心里嘀咕着。
　　"肯定特别好吃。"克鲁德也在心里嘀咕着，然
后他故意大声叫了起来。
　　小男孩儿被吓了一跳，手里的冰激凌一下掉在了
地上。"哇——"
　　"计谋成功。"克鲁德欢呼起来。

艾克立马朝着掉在地上的冰激凌冲了过去，他的
舌头已经准备好要舔上去了。
　　"哇——"艾克叼起掉在地上的圆筒冰激凌，他
抬头看了看大哭的小男孩儿，"哦，不，"艾克心
想，"他怎么感觉好像比我还要 卜 喵 呢！"

Ick scooted over to a short-short kid. Ick looked up.
The little boy licked at his cone. "Yum," thought Ick.

"Double yum," thought Crud and he barked louder
than he meant to. The frightened kid dropped his cone.
"WAAAAAHHHHHHH!!!"

"Get it," yelled Crud.

Ick dove for the cone, his tongue ready for the lick-lick-
licking.

"WAAAAAHHHHHHHH!!!" Ick grabbed the cone in his
mouth and looked up at the little boy. "Oh, no," thought Ick.
"He feels more *bleh* than me now."

So instead of woofing down the cone, Ick handed it to the boy. The kid grabbed the cone and went back to licking.

The tall, thin man poked his head out of the truck to see what all the crying was about. He spotted Ick and Crud. "Scram!" he yelled.

"Run!" said Crud.

The two raced around the big pink truck, behind the long park benches, along the bike path, and onto the sidewalk. They skidded to a stop.

"Sorry about the ice cream," said Crud.

"Not me," said Ick.

"No?" asked Crud.

"No," said Ick. "I no longer feel *bleh*. Now I feel like Ick."

"Like *ick*?" asked Crud.

"Yes," said Ick. "I feel like myself again."

"Great," said Crud. "Then let's go home, buddy."

于是克鲁德和艾克两人一路闻闻嗅嗅，
愉快地走回了家。

28

And off they went, sniff, sniff, sniffing all the way home.